KNOWABOUT

Weight

© 1994 Watts Books

Watts Books
96 Leonard Street
London EC2A 4RH

Franklin Watts Australia
14 Mars Road
Lane Cove
NSW 2066

ISBN: 0 7496 1667 9

Dewey Decimal Classification 530.8

10 9 8 7 6 5 4 3 2 1

A CIP catalogue record for this book
is available from the British Library.

Editor: Ruth Thomson
Assistant Editor: Annabel Martin

Design: Chloë Cheesman

Additional photographs: Eye Ubiquitous
© Paul Seheult 31; Quadrant Picture
Library 27; ZEFA 30.

Printed in Hong Kong

KNOWABOUT

Weight

Text: Henry Pluckrose
Photography: Chris Fairclough

Watts Books
London • New York • Sydney

Weight is a measuring word.
We weigh things to find out
how heavy they are.

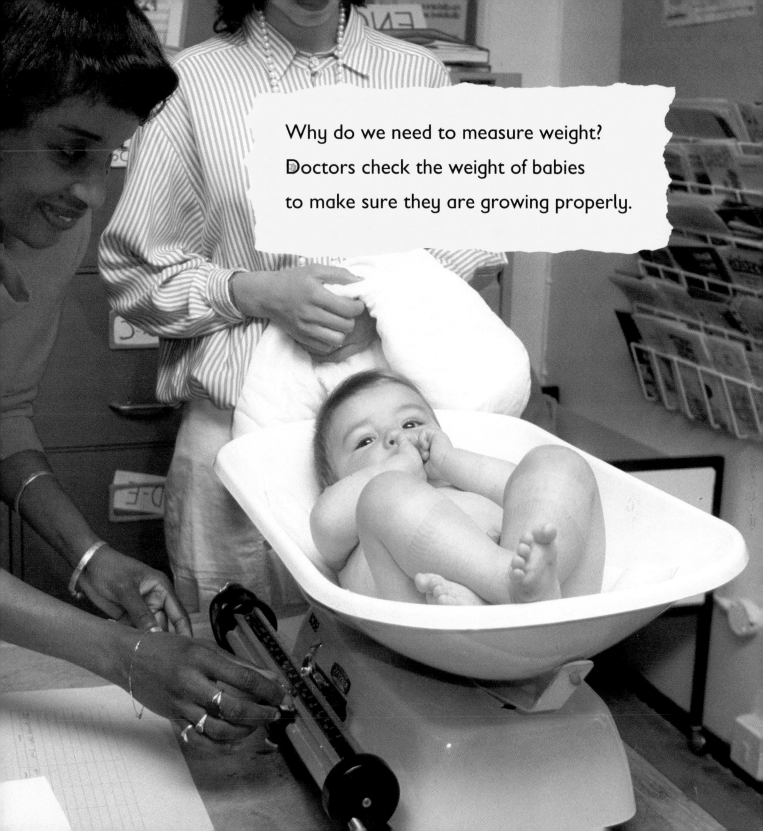

Why do we need to measure weight? Doctors check the weight of babies to make sure they are growing properly.

We weigh ingredients when we cook.
Only a small quantity of flour
is needed to make a cake.
Small quantities are weighed in grams.

This flour is being weighed
before it is sent to the bakery.
Large quantities of flour
are needed to make
all the loaves
sold in a supermarket.
Large quantities are weighed
in kilograms.

Everything weighs something –
even very light things
like a letter or a postcard.

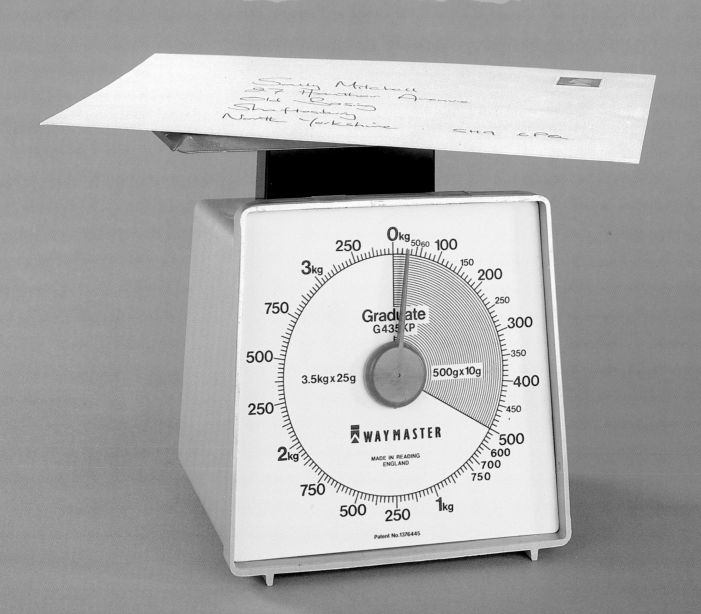

There are a lot of letters
and postcards
in these sacks.
Why are the sacks so heavy?

Sometimes we can guess
the weight of things.
Which do you think is lighter –
the feather or the stone?

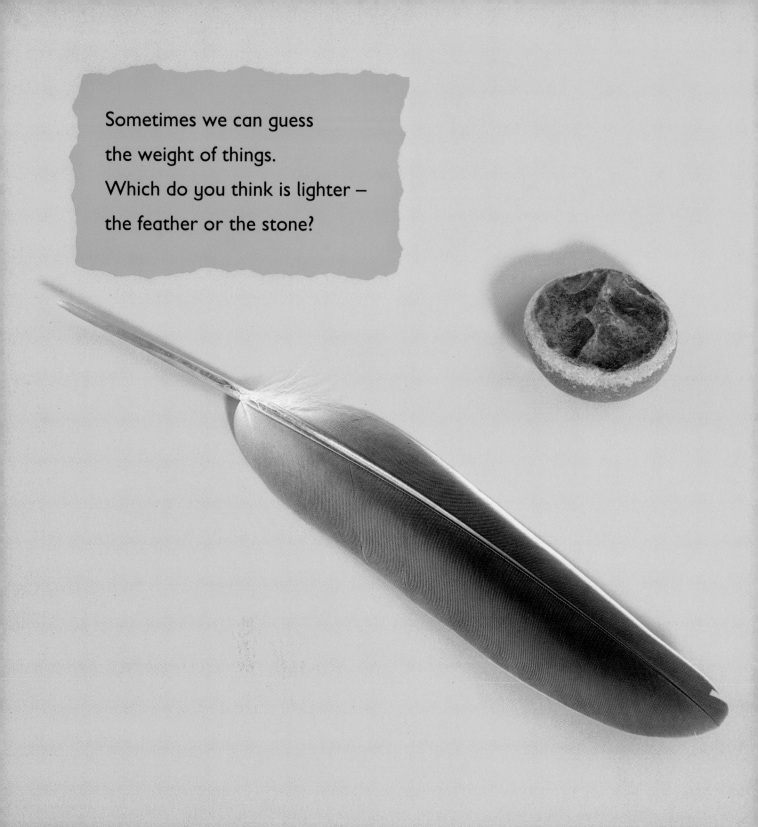

How could you make sure

that you have guessed correctly?

Guessing that one thing is heavier than another is not always easy.

How could you find out for certain which pile of tea is heavier?

You could put a stone in one pan of the balance.

Which is heavier – the tea bags …

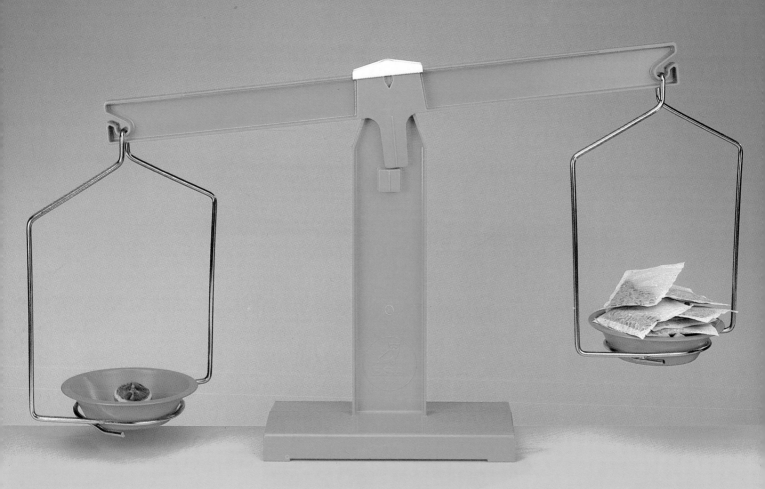

But stones are not all the same weight.

We use standard weights to measure heaviness.

1000 grams make one kilogram.

A kilogram of apples weighs exactly the same wherever you buy it.

If the apples were heavier than a kilogram the scales would not balance.

If the apples were lighter than a kilogram the scales would not balance either.

We can use scales to compare
the weight of different things.
A kilogram of apples is as heavy
as a kilogram of potatoes.

Would a kilogram of rice weigh more, less or the same as a kilogram of cheese?

It is important to know
how heavy things are.
Shopkeepers often weigh food
when they sell it.
We pay for the weight of food
that we buy.

Even when food is sold in packets, the weight of the contents is marked on the label.

Luggage is weighed at the airport before it is loaded on to a plane.

If a plane was overloaded
it could not fly safely.

Lorries and vans must not be overloaded either.

This small lorry could not carry ...

something as heavy as this!

Crane operators have to be sure that the crane is strong enough to lift the weight of the goods it is moving.

Notices next to weak bridges tell drivers
the weight that the bridges can carry.
Very heavy lorries cannot travel
over this bridge.
The roadway would not support
their weight.

Some people lift heavy weights as a sport.

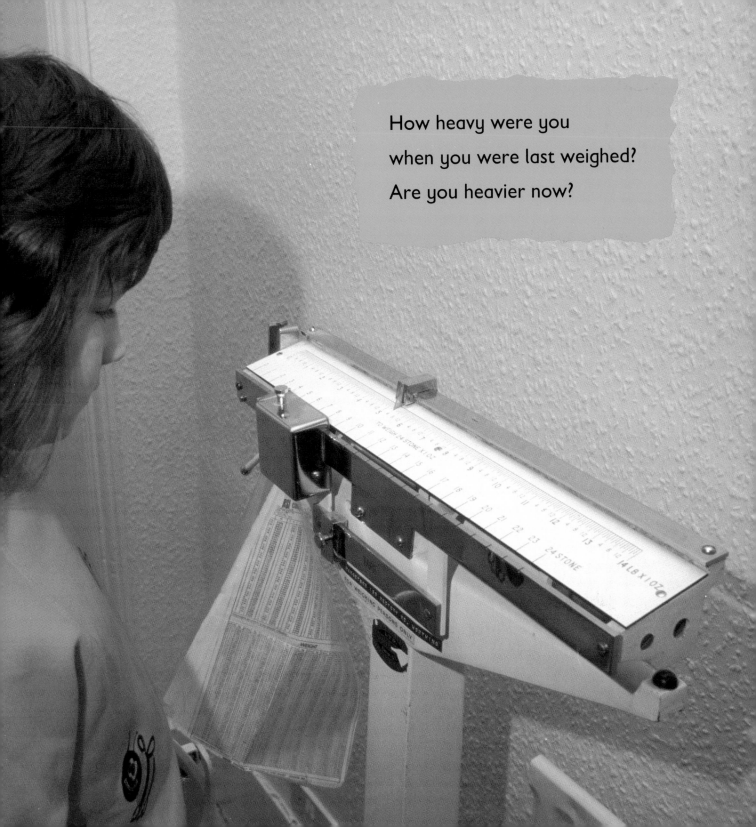

How heavy were you
when you were last weighed?
Are you heavier now?

About this book

This book is designed for use in the home, playgroup, kindergarten
and infant school.
The parents can share the book with young children. Its aim is to bring
into focus some of the elements of life and living which are too
often taken for granted. To develop fully, all young children need
to have their understanding of the world deepened and the
language they use to express their ideas extended. This book, and
others in the series, takes the everyday things of the child's world
and explores them, harnessing curiosity and wonder in a
purposeful way.

For those working with young children each book is designed to be
used both as a picture book, which explores ideas and concepts,
and as a starting point to talk and exploration. The pictures have
been selected because they are of interest in themselves and also
because they include elements which will promote enquiry. Talk
can lead to displays of items and pictures collected by children and
teacher. Pictures and collages can be made by the children
themselves.

Everything in our environment is of interest to the growing child.
The purpose of these books is to extend and develop that interest.

Henry Pluckrose